ARCHBISHOP THOMAS AND KING HENRY II

Tom Corfe

GENERAL EDITOR TREVOR CAIRNS

CAMBRIDGE UNIVERSITY PRESS
CAMBRIDGE
LONDON · NEW YORK · MELBOURNE

Drawings by Valerie Bell
Maps and diagrams by Oxford Illustrators

front cover: *The murder of Archbishop Thomas in 1170, painted about twenty or thirty years later. This is part of a picture in a manuscript now in the British Museum. Another painting from the same book is on page 43.*

back cover: *Henry II as he appears in a book made about sixty years after his death. Another page from this manuscript is shown on page 24.*

opposite: *Archbishop Thomas, from a thirteenth-century window in Canterbury Cathedral.*

Published by the Syndics of the Cambridge University Press
The Pitt Building, Trumpington Street, Cambridge CB2 1RP
Bentley House, 200 Euston Road, London NW1 2DB
32 East 57th Street, New York, NY 10022, USA
296 Beaconsfield Parade, Middle Park, Melbourne 3206, Australia

© Cambridge University Press 1975

Library of Congress Catalogue Card Number: 74-14442

ISBN 0 521 20646 6

First published 1975

Photoset and printed in Malta by St Paul's Press Ltd

The author and publisher would like to thank the following for permission to reproduce illustrations:
front cover, back cover, pages 6 (manuscript), 15 (Grim), 18 (lecture), 24 (manuscript), 36 (miniatures), 40, 42, 43, 46 (pilgrims), The British Library Board, 5, Pitkin Pictorial, Ltd; 6 (boss and window), 10, 11; 12 (crypt), 44, 45, National Monuments Record; 6 (casket), 21 (Monkwearmouth), A. F. Kersting: 8, 26, The Master and Fellows of Trinity College, Cambridge; 9, Colin Dudley; 12 (painting), 14, 15 (murder), 20 (tapestry), 36 (mitre), Victoria and Albert Museum, Crown copyright; mitre by permission of the Cardinal Archbishop of Westminster; 18 (beating), Dean and Chapter of Durham Cathedral; 19, 23, 41 (Pontigny), Archives Photographiques, Paris; 20 (Lanfranc), 47 (window), Bodleian Library; 20 (William), Phaidon Press; 21 (chapel and abbey), 25 (Berkhamsted), 27 (Dover and Orford), Department of the Environment, Crown copyright; 25 (drawing), 28, Alan Sorrell; 27, Scarborough Corporation; 29, 30 (tallies), 34, Public Record Office; 30 and 31 (coins), Ashmolean Museum; 36 (chasuble), 41 (Sens), French Government Tourist Board; 33 (writ), Dean and Chapter of Westminster Abbey; 37 (miniature), Cambridge University Library; 37 (photograph), Radio Times Hulton Picture Library; 39, Cambridge University Department of Aerial Photography; 41 (miniature), Mansell Collection; 46 (badge), Cambridge University, Museum of Archaeology and Ethnology; 48 (Irving and Eliot), Mander and Mitchenson Theatre Collection; 48 (Burton), Paramount Pictures.
The translations from lives of St Thomas are based on those made by George Greenaway, in *The Life and Death of Thomas Becket* (Folio Society, 1961). The translation from the Anglo-Saxon Chronicle on pp. 23–4 is based on that in *English Historical Documents*, Vol. II (Eyre and Spottiswoode) by Miss S. I. Tucker.

Contents

1 The death of the archbishop

In the year 1170, on 29 December, at about the hour of evening service, Archbishop Thomas of Canterbury was killed by four knights within his own cathedral.

Everyone knew that for seven years the archbishop had been quarrelling bitterly with King Henry. The four knights were loyal servants of the king. They and everyone else believed they were acting on the king's behalf and at his wish.

The violent killing of the foremost churchman of all England, and in such a holy place, horrified all good Christians. Archbishop Thomas seemed a martyr, slain at the bidding of a cruel enemy of God's Church, and very soon he was proclaimed a saint. All Christendom wanted to know how and why this dreadful deed had happened.

Eyewitnesses and artists

Many people were there when the archbishop was slain. There were some of his friends and servants, visitors who had come from afar to see him, monks of the cathedral, townsfolk of Canterbury; and of course there were those four murderous knights and their followers.

Perhaps on that December evening it was too dark for any of them to see everything clearly. But the gloomy cavern of the church was lit by scores of flickering candles; twenty-four of them, mounted on a gilded circle, hung like a glittering crown over the choir stalls of the monks. Before long the artists of the day, who may well have talked to eyewitnesses, were painting their idea of the scene. One such picture, in a *psalter* or copy of the psalms made only twenty or thirty years after the crime, is now in the British Museum and is shown on the cover of this book. The artist has been careful with most of the details, but he is wrong about one thing, perhaps deliberately. To make clear what a terrible crime has been committed he actually shows the archbishop kneeling at the high altar itself,

although we know for a fact that he died not at that very holy spot but in a side chapel with his back against a pillar. That chapel is now called The Martyrdom, and although the cathedral has been rebuilt the spot has been remembered and it is marked by an inscription on the wall.

On the next page you can see some of the ways in which artists over the next century or so showed the murder. It was a favourite subject for paintings on church walls or in illustrated books, for enamel caskets and stained-glass windows, and for stone carvings like the one in the roof of Exeter Cathedral. These are only a few of those still left out of thousands of pictures of the scene that medieval artists produced.

The martyrdom of St Thomas

top left: *A fourteenth-century manuscript in the British Museum.*
top right: *An enamel casket in Hereford Cathedral Library (thirteenth century).*
bottom left: *A window in Christ Church Cathedral, Oxford. (fourteenth century).*
bottom right: *A roof-boss in Exeter Cathedral (fourteenth century).*

The drawing on page 4 shows how a modern artist sees what happened; it is based on all the reports of the eyewitnesses.

Several of the archbishop's friends and followers wrote detailed descriptions of the crime as they had seen it. William fitzStephen, who had long served and helped him as priest, secretary and friend, has left us his story of what happened in Canterbury on that wintry day more than 800 years ago. He tells how the four knights met the archbishop in an inner chamber of his palace; how they demanded that Thomas give way to the king's wishes, how Thomas refused and the argument got fiercer:

'Do you realise that you owe everything to the king?'

'Certainly not; we must render to the king the things that are the king's and to God the things that are God's.'

At this, says William fitzStephen, Reginald and his fellow knights growled at him and ground their teeth in rage. But the righteous Thomas, brave as a lion, showed no terror.

The angry knights left. But they did not go far. Outside in the courtyard they gathered their followers, barred the gate against interference, and put on their heavy armour. William fitzStephen continues:

We heard the cries of the crowds, who had seen armed men in the city marching under orders towards the archbishop's palace. Then said the monks, a good many of whom now stood around him, 'My lord, go into the church.' 'I certainly will not', he answered. 'Have no fear; most of you monks are more timid and faint-hearted than you should be.' To this they would not agree. Some took hold of him, pulled him to his feet, and pushed him forward. Others tried to persuade him to go. It had been his intention anyway to go to evening service, and the monks were already saying vespers, so he went, ordering the cross of the Lord to be carried in front of him.

Palace, monastery, cathedral

It is time, like good detectives, to look more closely at the scene of the crime.

The archbishop's palace, where Thomas argued with the knights and where the timid monks urged him to seek safety in the church, has long ago disappeared. Like most great houses of its day it was essentially a single hall on an upper floor, entered from an outside stairway. One or two private rooms were partitioned off at each end of the hall, and in one of these the angry meeting took place. Below, the ground floor was taken up with cellars and storerooms. The artist's drawing on page 9 shows what it may have looked like.

The palace was just outside the monastery. Like many cathedrals of the Middle Ages, Canterbury was served by monks of the Order of St Benedict. For them, the archbishop's cathedral was the church where they worshipped day and night. Very little of the monastery remains, but we know a great deal about what it looked like.

It seems that about 1150 the Canterbury monks needed a new water system, and the fine drawing on the next page was made for the guidance of the builders planning the pipes and sewers. It shows at the top the cathedral church itself. Below it (actually on the north side; nowadays we usually show north at the top of the plan, but this was drawn the other way up) the planner shows the *cloisters*, the covered walk with its rows of arches around the green *garth*. All about the cloisters of every monastery were the buildings where the monks lived and worked. Their Latin names are written on the plan: the *cellarium* or storeroom; *refectorium*, or eating-hall (with kitchens beside it); and *dormitorium*, or sleeping-place. In another courtyard to the left the plan shows the new water-tower and wash-place that was to be at the centre of the system; later it was added to and altered, but you can still

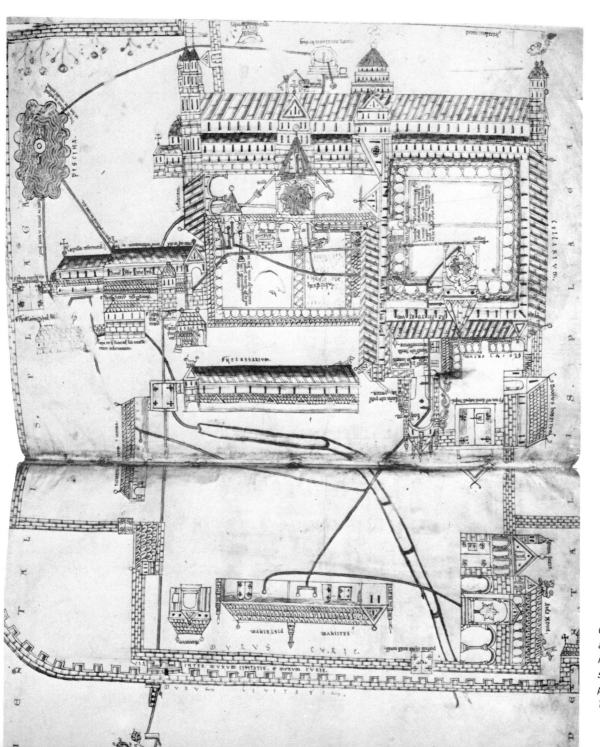

Canterbury Cathedral and monastery, with its new water system, shown in a plan drawn about 1150.

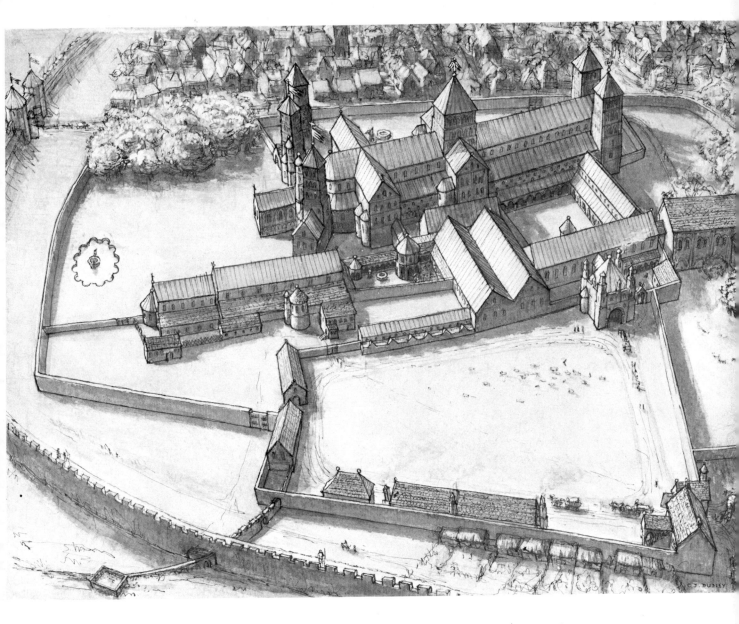

A modern artist's picture of the same buildings as in the plan opposite. Pick out the water tower that was at the heart of the system, near the middle of each picture. Pages 7 and 10 will help you to sort out the different buildings and their purposes. Notice that today's artist has shown one building that is not on the plan because it was outside the monastery: it is the Archbishop's Palace at the far right.

9

pick out the round Norman arches of the original tower in the picture on the right. Also there are the *herbarium*, or herb garden, and the *necessarium* or latrine. Further to the left are the buildings of the *infirmarium*, where elderly or sick monks lived under conditions rather easier than those of their brethren who had to obey the strict rules.

Facing the twelfth-century plan, you can see how a modern artist has used it (and other evidence) to make a drawing of what the monastery looked like.

The peaceful buildings of the monastery could be reached from the inner room of the archbishop's palace by going down a stair and through a door into the cloister. Thomas was led by his frightened companions around the cloister and into the church itself. You can follow his path, and that of the knights, on the plan opposite.

The cathedral church that they now entered was mostly destroyed by fire four years after the murder. The fine building we can see today rose upon its blackened ruins. But we know about the church, just as we know about the monastery. In this case, our information comes from a book written by a monk of Canterbury called Gervase. He tells us what the church was like when it was newly completed, about the year 1130. Some of what he describes is illustrated on the water-

above left: *Southwell Cathedral.*

above: *Water tower, Canterbury Cathedral.*

far right: *St Augustine's Chair, Canterbury Cathedral.*

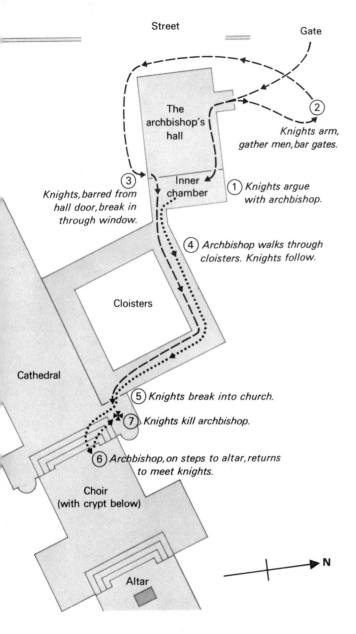

Street

Gate

The archbishop's hall

② *Knights arm, gather men, bar gates.*

③ *Knights, barred from hall door, break in through window.*

Inner chamber

① *Knights argue with archbishop.*

④ *Archbishop walks through cloisters. Knights follow.*

Cloisters

Cathedral

⑤ *Knights break into church.*

⑦ *Knights kill archbishop.*

⑥ *Archbishop, on steps to altar, returns to meet knights.*

Choir (with crypt below)

Altar

N

system plan. He mentions the central tower with a gilded cherub on its summit, the two lofty towers on the right with their gilded pinnacles, the massive walls with rather small windows. Though we cannot see today the church that

Gervase described, we can look at pictures of others built about the same time that fit his description well. The picture opposite shows the nave at Southwell Minster in Nottinghamshire, now itself a cathedral. Once Canterbury must have looked much like this.

Inside, Gervase describes the lines of pillars stretching along the nave and choir of the church, linked by round arches. It was solid and massive, as Norman buildings usually were. Above the line of arches ran a passageway, the *triforium*; and above that, to give more light, was another line of windows, the *clerestory*. Above it all, worshippers gazing upwards would see majestic paintings decorating the ceiling.

If you went from the entrance at the west end of the church towards the altar, you would mount a flight of steps into the choir (as you do still today). There were more steps at the altar itself; and beyond the altar, above yet another flight, was the archbishop's throne. The throne above was made soon after Archbishop Thomas's day, and it may have been a copy of the earlier one, lost in the great fire. That older throne, on

left: *St Paul and the viper, (Acts, ch. 28) a copy by E. W. Tristram of a twelfth-century painting that can still be seen at Canterbury.*

below: *The Norman crypt.*

which Thomas himself had been solemnly enthroned with pomp and ceremony in 1162, was perhaps the very chair made for Saint Augustine, the first Archbishop of Canterbury.

Some parts of the church that Gervase wrote of and Thomas knew still remain. They have survived the fire and the centuries, and you can see two pictures of them on this page. Beneath the choir was the *crypt*, below the flights of steps leading up to the altar. It is still packed with the columns carved by the Norman craftsmen of nearly 900 years ago, with chapels, tombs, and shrines for sacred relics. Above the crypt, leading off the rebuilt choir, you can still find some of the arches and chapels of Thomas's church, even some of the paintings with which it was so richly decorated, like that of St Paul.

When Archbishop Thomas was murdered in 1170 the cathedral was still a new building, of clean-cut stone and brightly painted plaster. With his little procession of agitated monks, anxious to get as far as possible from the angry hubbub behind them, the archbishop made his way into the church by way of the door from the cloisters. William fitzStephen's story goes on:

The monks, trembling and upset by so strange and great a tumult, broke off their singing of vespers and came out of the choir to meet the archbishop as he entered the church. He was going towards the altar, further up the church, and had already mounted four steps, when lo! at the door from the cloister through which he had come there appeared first Reginald fitzUrse, clad in a suit of mail and with drawn sword, shouting 'Here now to me, king's men!' A moment later he was joined by his three comrades, similarly clad, head and body in full armour, everything covered but their eyes and with naked swords in their hands. There were a great many others, without suits of mail, but armed, their retainers and friends.

The knights

Who were these fearsome men, heavily armoured, weapons in their hands, bursting into the house of God?

Here is Reginald fitzUrse. His name means 'bear's son', and his long wooden shield carries his badge; otherwise it would be very difficult to tell who he was. His main garment is a heavy *hauberk*, a coat of mail made of iron rings skilfully interlocked. It is a costly and valued garment; perhaps Reginald has inherited it from his father. Its sleeves are loose-fitting; some knights prefer full-length sleeves, but unless these are very carefully made they can make moving an arm or swinging a sword difficult. Over Reginald's head and neck is a *coif* of mail, and under his hauberk he wears a long coat of linen or leather. For battle, he would wear also leggings of mail. His helmet is beaten out of a single piece of iron, with a nose-piece rivetted on. His sword is a long-bladed heavy cutting weapon.

Reginald's companions that day were William de Traci, Hugh of Morville and Richard Brito. Like Reginald they were ready to serve the king in battle when they were summoned, each with a band of armed followers and servants. But they were not just warriors. Each was a feudal baron, holding land from the king in return for services to him, managing his own estates and keeping peace and order among the folk of his villages. They would ride abroad on the king's business, bearing his orders and messages, carrying out his instructions. Hugh was a great landowner in the north country and a justice, whose duty it was to see that men behaved well and kept the king's laws through wide stretches of Cumberland and Northumberland. Reginald and William had both once served Thomas himself and held lands from him, in the days before he became archbishop. Richard had been for many years a close friend of the king's younger brother. All had been often at

13

Murder

Archbishop Thomas faced the men who had come to seize him. William fitzStephen's account goes on:

> The good archbishop, putting his whole trust in the Lord, turned back and came down the steps, forbidding the monks to close the door, saying, 'Far be it from us to turn the church of God into a fortress. Let anyone who wishes come into the church. God's will be done.' If he had wished the archbishop could easily have turned away and saved himself by flight. It was evening, the long winter night was approaching, and the crypt was near at hand where there were many dark and winding passages. There was also another door near, through which he could have climbed by a spiral staircase to the arched chamber in the roof of the church. But none of these ways of escape would he take.

We can imagine the archbishop, tall and imposing in his robes, facing the knights. We know that he was well over six feet at a time when most men were shorter than they are today, and that he had a fierce beak of a nose. He wore a mitre on his head, and over his robes of linen and silk the *pallium*, the embroidered strip of cloth given by the pope as his badge of authority as an archbishop; it was just so that artists later painted him on many a church wall.

Behind him stood Edward Grim, a clerk visiting Canterbury who was caught up by accident in the events of the day. It is Grim who stands close to the archbishop in most pictures of the murder. He was not a monk, but as you can see the top of his head was shaved in priestly fashion because he, like most educated men of the day, had passed into the lower ranks of the clergy. It is Edward Grim himself who now takes up the story:

the court of King Henry ever since he had been crowned, sixteen years before. They were loyal men, ever ready to do the king's bidding.

That Christmas, four days before, they had been attending the king beyond the Channel at his hall of Bures in Normandy.

Christmas had not been a very happy time for King Henry. He did not like what he heard of Archbishop Thomas's doings in England. The news was so upsetting that he had flown into a rage. 'What miserable cowards I have in my court!' he said. 'Is there no one who will free me from this low-born priest?'

Perhaps it was meant to be a hint. Perhaps it was just thoughtless bad temper. The four knights thought it was obvious what the king their master wanted. They hurried from Henry's court. Before anyone else realised what was afoot they had taken ship across the Channel to England, determined either to seize the archbishop and make him the king's prisoner, or to kill him in the attempt.

Edward Grim.

right: *A thirteenth-century painting of the murder, now much damaged, on the wall of South Newington Church, Oxfordshire.*

Inspired by fury the knights called out, 'Where is Thomas Becket, traitor to the king and realm?' As he answered not, they cried out more furiously, 'Where is the archbishop?'

At this he answered in a clear voice, 'I am here, no traitor to the king, but a priest. Why do you seek me?'

'Absolve', they cried, 'those you have excommunicated, and restore their powers to those you have dismissed.'

He answered, 'There has been no satisfaction, and I will not absolve them.'

'Then you shall die', they cried, 'and get what you deserve.'

'I am ready', he replied, 'to die for my Lord, so that with my blood the Church may obtain liberty and peace. But in the name of Almighty God I forbid you to harm my people.'

Then they laid hands on him, pulling and dragging him that they might kill him outside the church, or carry him away a prisoner. When he could not be forced away one knight waved his sword over his head. Seeing the hour at hand he inclined his neck like a man at prayer; and joining his hands he lifted them up and commended his cause and that of the Church of God to St Mary and to the blessed martyr Denis. Scarce had he said the words than the wicked knight, fearing that he might be rescued by the people and escape alive, leapt upon him suddenly and wounded him on the head; and by the same blow he wounded the arm of him who tells this tale, for he, when the others (both monks and clerks) had fled, stuck close to the saintly archbishop and held him in his arms till the one he interposed was almost cut off.

Then he received a second blow on the head, but still stood firm. At the third blow he fell on his knees and elbows, offering himself a living victim and saying in a low voice, 'For the Name of Jesus and the protection of the Church I am ready to embrace death.' Then the third knight inflicted a terrible wound as he lay by which the sword was shattered against the pavement, so that the blood and the brains dyed the floor of the church. A clerk who had entered with the knights put his foot on the neck of the holy priest, calling out to the others, 'Let us away, knights; he will rise no more.'

2 Archbishop Thomas and his Church

What sort of man was Archbishop Thomas? If we know more of the victim, perhaps we shall understand better why he was murdered.

Thomas of London

Thomas was just past his fifty-second birthday when he was killed. He was born in London, in the street called Cheapside, on 21 December 1118. His father was a merchant who had come from his home in Normandy to settle in the busy trading centre, a successful man respected by his fellow-citizens. Of course most of his neighbours would be English, and Thomas probably spoke their language as well as his own Norman-French. But unlike many of the other young men about him as he grew up, Thomas would have no difficulty in talking easily with the Norman rulers of England, the great barons and the bishops.

In fact many of the most important dealings of Thomas's career would take place in a third language, the Latin that he was taught when first he went to school. It was the language of much business, of everything to do with the Church and government, of books and learned discussion.

Thomas's father was known as Gilbert Becket, and Thomas

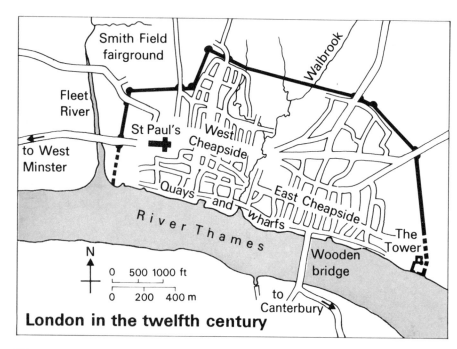

London in the twelfth century

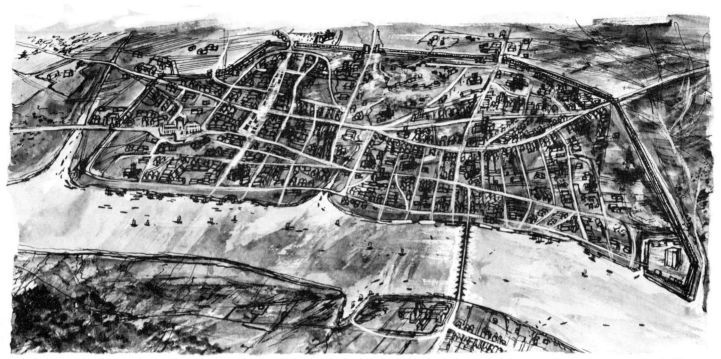

would sometimes be called by his father's surname. But surnames were not then common, and once he left home he would usually be known simply as Thomas of London. He was hardly ever called 'Becket' in his days of greatness; only in the last moments of his life, when the knights burst in to kill him, did one call out 'Where is Thomas Becket?', deliberately insulting the mighty archbishop by reminding him of his humble London birth. Thomas ignored that call.

The city

William fitzStephen, in his account of the archbishop's life, describes the London in which he grew up. It was tiny compared with the London of today, with no more people than a small country town, perhaps 15,000 of them at most. But to the men of the twelfth century it was a wealthy, proud, far-famed city. The plan opposite and the drawing above show what it must have looked like.

In the narrow streets and along the busy quaysides lining the river below the wooden bridge that spanned the Thames swarmed merchants, craftsmen, shopkeepers, priests and scholars. Overlooking the warehouses and markets was the strong stone keep of King William the Conqueror's Tower, gleaming white, reminding the Londoners that they were under the control and protection of the Norman King, whose sheriff held it with a force of soldiers. Two other castles, which have long since disappeared, guarded the city on the west, where the road led out along the *strand*, or riverside, to the royal palace and abbey of Westminster. A high wall, the old Roman wall much rebuilt, ringed the northern side of the city. It had towers and double gateways at intervals, and beyond it there were houses and gardens, pastures and meadows, water-mills and rich cornfields, woodland swarming with game, and a great marsh upon which in winter young men like Thomas skated with animal shin-bones lashed to their feet, pushing themselves along with iron-shod poles.

Within the walls, among the well-paved busy streets were many churches, thirteen great ones served by monks and 126 smaller parish churches. There were markets for meat, fish and poultry, cookshops, eating-houses and wine-cellars. There were wells and aqueducts and sewers to supply water and clean the city. There were schools, including the one in St Paul's Cathedral that Thomas probably attended.

17

A lecture at Paris, as painted in a fourteenth-century manuscript.

right: *Punishment for a schoolboy, shown in a twelfth-century manuscript.*

Schools

Thomas first went to school with the monks at the Priory of Merton in Surrey, and he began the hard life of a scholar there when he was about ten years old. For four or five years he rose at 6 a.m. to spend the day in bleak cloisters learning how to write and speak good Latin, how to read and understand the books left by Roman authors of long ago, and how to worship God in the priory church.

In becoming a scholar, Thomas was becoming also a clerk, entering into the lowest ranks of the all-embracing Church. For the rest of his life he could claim that he was set aside from ordinary uneducated men, for he understood not only the Latin language but the much greater mysteries of religion. It might be that he would go on to the dedicated, humble life of a monk himself; or he might turn to being a parish priest, serving and guiding simple villagers; or he might choose not

to go further along the path of religion but to put his learning at the service of some merchant or noble or royal official. But whatever course he chose he would remain a clerk, set aside from other men; and Thomas never forgot that, in his personal life, he must behave as a good churchman and avoid any conduct that might seem a sin in the eyes of God.

Young Thomas enjoyed learning, and he was an able scholar. He went on to the school of St Paul's, and there he learnt the arts of argument and public speaking, how to write long thoughtful essays and compose verses. It helped to make him a quick thinker and a shrewd debater.

There were two ways in which his education might be carried yet further. The word 'university' was not used in Thomas's day, but the most famous teachers and learned lecturers were to be found gathered together at Paris. That city was perhaps ten times the size of London, and students came from all over western Europe to crowd into its churches,

Peter Abelard, carved on a pillar in a French church.

even into the cathedral of Notre Dame itself, listening to lectures and taking part in debates.

This was an exciting time of new discovery and new thinking. Everyone in Paris was asking questions, questions about Man, about the Universe, about God; and sometimes the answers seemed new and strange. Eagerly they sought wisdom by reading and re-reading the writings of long-dead Greek and Roman thinkers. They even translated the learned books of Arab scholars and scientists in the search for knowledge and understanding.

All this new thinking, and particularly thinking about Christianity and its importance, spread from the shrewd and clever teachers in Paris to the thousands of students who came to listen to them. With the students the new thinking returned to their homelands, and in time it had effect on the lives of ordinary folk. Religion, the thoughtful and serious worship of God, came to matter more and more for everybody. Men everywhere were anxious to serve God as well as serving their feudal overlords.

The most famous of the teachers at Paris was Peter Abelard, who had given up the life of a knight because he loved learning and teaching. We must always ask questions, Peter taught; we must never blindly trust what others tell us. Only by debate and enquiry can we come nearer the real truth. Perhaps Thomas of London was one of the hundreds who sat on the straw-covered floor of a Paris church to listen, and took part in these important arguments. What was God like, they wondered. How could one best serve Him? Could one be faithful to God and His Church (and to the pope as head of that Church) and still serve an earthly king like Louis of France? It was exciting for a student from England to be talking about all these things with the wisest men in Christendom and studying the precious books so carefully copied out by busy monks and scribes. Soon many of the Englishmen would be guiding simple, ordinary folk along the right path of Christian worship.

Thomas enjoyed many months studying in Paris. But before he entered on his adult life, there was one more step. He must learn how to be a gentleman, something not usually possible for a merchant's son. But Gilbert Becket was no common merchant; he seems to have been prosperous, and of course he was a Norman, so that he often dealt with Norman nobles when they were visiting town. He arranged for Thomas to spend some time as squire in the household of one of these. There, while serving his master, he learnt how to ride and hawk and hunt and joust, how to eat and dress and behave like a member of the ruling class.

In the end, Thomas was in most ways a highly educated young man. It remained to find a place in life where he might use his learning and ability. After three dull years as clerk to a London alderman his opportunity came.

The Archbishop of Canterbury happened to come from the same part of Normandy as Gilbert Becket. Once again the old man was able to help the son he had educated so well. Thomas was about twenty-five when it was arranged that he should enter the archbishop's household.

Archbishop Lanfranc and Archbishop Theobald

Becoming clerk to Archbishop Theobald meant that Thomas would be very near the centre of English affairs. The archbishops of Canterbury had been close to the king ever since Augustine had converted Ethelbert of Kent. The link had been made stronger in the tenth century when King Edgar and St Dunstan had co-operated in a great religious revival and reorganization.

Fifty years before Thomas was born, William the Norman (King Henry II's great-grandfather) had made himself King of the English. Just as he was determined to place Norman barons throughout the country, each holding land from the Norman king in return for service to him, so he set Norman bishops and abbots in all the most important posts of the Church. Stigand, Archbishop of Canterbury, was one of those Englishmen whom William drove out of office.

Stigand's replacement was an elderly Italian named Lanfranc, who had spent many years as abbot of the monastery of Bec in Normandy. Everybody respected Lanfranc as a wise and sensible man. He knew all about the new ideas that were already becoming popular in Europe, ideas about the kind of life that Christians should lead and the part the Church should play in men's lives. The Anglo-Saxon churchmen, he felt, had shown too little interest in such ideas.

Lanfranc set out to change the organization and customs of the English Church. He made it clear that he, as archbishop, was also *primate*, leader of the whole Church in England; and that all churchmen must follow his rulings. Frequently he summoned his bishops and abbots together so that they could plan reforms. They put a stop to the selling of positions in the Church, and they ruled that priests should never marry but must devote their whole lives to God's work.

The new rules for the behaviour of churchmen were soon accepted by bishops and priests throughout the land, so great was the crusading vigour and missionary drive with which Lanfranc urged them, and so well was he supported by his powerful master, King William. Lanfranc served Christianity well, helping to make it an important part of people's lives; and he also served King William well, both as his foremost adviser and as the head of his Church. The bishops took their places among the great feudal barons and their share in governing the country.

Just as the barons built castles, so Lanfranc and the other Norman bishops encouraged the building of strong stone churches throughout the country. Some of the Saxon churches that they found were quite large and built of stone (like Monkwearmouth, on the right) but most were small wooden buildings. The Normans quickly showed that they could build much stronger, larger, better lit churches, fit for the more important place they were now to occupy in men's lives. They were buildings rich with painting and carving, the busy centres of activity in every village. On the opposite page you can also see two of the churches the Normans built.

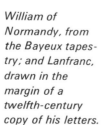

William of Normandy, from the Bayeux tapestry; and Lanfranc, drawn in the margin of a twelfth-century copy of his letters.

far left: Monkwear-mouth church tower, in Sunderland, was built in Anglo-Saxon times. It is tall and narrow, with uneven masonry.

left: St John's Chapel, built in the time of William the Conqueror inside the Tower of London, is much more massive.

below: Buildwas Abbey, a later Norman church, built in the time of Archbishop Thomas.

The Norman kings and some of their archbishops

William I	William II	Henry I	Stephen	Henry II

10|66 10|70   1087 10|89 10|93   11|00   11|09   11|35 11|38   11|54   1161| 11|62   11|70

Lanfranc   Anselm   Theobald   Thomas

One of the first of Lanfranc's new buildings was his own cathedral at Canterbury. There had been a fine Anglo-Saxon cathedral, but it had been burnt down in 1067. Lanfranc's new church was built in rather a hurry, but over the next fifty years it was added to by other archbishops and by the priors who, under them, headed the monastery. This was the church shown on page 9, the church that Thomas knew when he served Archbishop Theobald.

Lanfranc and King William had the same purpose, to impose Norman ways on the people, so they worked well together. Lanfranc's successor, Anselm, another former abbot of Bec, was a saintly man who never got on with William II or Henry I. He found them too interfering and overbearing, and had to defend the rights of the Church against them. Archbishop Theobald was yet another former abbot of Bec. He was a learned and saintly man like Anselm, but he hoped to work with the king as Lanfranc had, and not against him.

But when Theobald became archbishop in 1138 times were difficult. The country was tangled in civil war, and the archbishop was always trying to arrange a peaceful settlement or seeing that the warlike barons on both sides treated churchmen with proper respect. In these times of trouble many looked to the Church for help and so it became ever more important a part of people's lives.

Moreover, many of the powerful and wicked men who made themselves rich by bullying weaker neighbours during the wars thought it wise to befriend the Church. If they gave it money, or set up new monasteries, the Church might protect them from their enemies and the consequences of their misdeeds both in this world and the next. So the Church grew richer and stronger than ever.

With Archbishop Theobald, or on his behalf, Thomas met all the great men of the kingdom and beyond it. There were missions to France to be carried out, and even as far as Rome to confer with the pope, head of the whole western Church. He spent some time in Italy to study Church law, for the archbishop and the Church's courts were constantly being called on to deliver justice and settle disputes.

Throughout the years that he served the archbishop Thomas was mixing with some of the ablest and cleverest men in all England, for many other ex-scholars were gathered into Theobald's household. Educated, hard-working, conscientious, enthusiastic servants of God, the clerks, priests and lawyers who surrounded the archbishop were well aware of their duties as leaders of the Church. Sometimes they must have thought to themselves that they might well do better at running the country than the king and his quarrelling barons. They knew too that they were members of a much wider organization, for their Church spread far beyond national boundaries. Many of the archbishop's followers came from abroad, and many English churchmen were to be found throughout Europe. Every churchman owed loyalty to the pope as well as to the king; and it was while Thomas was in Theobald's service that, for the only time in history, an Englishman was actually elected as pope.

For ten years Thomas served his master well. Tall and thin, haughty, forceful in argument and vigorous in action, he was often at Theobald's side to help and advise. Late in 1154 he was nearing his thirty-sixth birthday. He had been made Archdeacon of Canterbury, and most men thought him a promising churchman. Perhaps, in time, if all went well, he might himself become a bishop.

3 King Henry and his England

Late in 1154 Henry II became King of England. We have no reliable portraits of him. Perhaps the best is the much repaired figure on his tomb at Fontevrault in France, shown here. But we have vivid descriptions from those who served him, and from some of those who disliked him; King Henry made an unforgettable impression on all who met him and worked with him.

He was above average height, but because he was broad-built and bull-necked, with long arms and bowed legs from much riding, he looked short and solid and stocky. He had reddish hair and a spotty red face that rapidly turned an even more violent shade when he lost his temper, which he quite often did. Above all he was energetic, always on the move, making quick and sound decisions, and acting with great speed. Nobody could tell in advance what he might do. Courtiers and knights, waking at dawn, would find that everyone and everything was being packed hurriedly on to mules and horses ready for the whole court to make a swift move. Henry was always wakeful and active, whether he was working or relaxing. He rode, hunted, talked, fought, ate, argued, hawked until he tired everyone else out. He could read, when he had time, and even write; and he enjoyed arguing with men of learning. He hoped above all to preserve order and peace among his subjects, and he disliked and resented any who opposed him. Some thought him a tyrant who destroyed much that was honoured by time and tradition, but none doubted his ability to plan and to command men. Though he was sometimes thoughtless, sometimes angry, sometimes foolish, he was not usually a cruel man.

The state of England

When Henry came to the throne Englishmen welcomed him as a deliverer after years of trouble. The monks of Peterborough recorded their memories of the late King Stephen's time:

When the traitors understood that he was a mild man and gentle and good, and did not exact the full penalties of the law, every powerful man built his castles and held them against him, and they filled the land full of castles. They oppressed the wretched people of the country fearfully with their castle-building. When the castles were built they filled them with devils and evil men. Then, both by night and day, they took those that they thought had any goods, both men and women, and put them in prison and tortured them with unspeakable tortures to extort gold and silver; no martyrs were ever so tortured as they were. I have neither the ability nor the power to tell of all the horrors nor all the torments they inflicted upon the wretched people of this country; and this state of things lasted the nineteen years while Stephen was king, and ever grew worse and worse. They levied taxes on the villages every so often and called it 'protection money'. When the wretched people had no more to give they robbed and burned all the villages so that

23

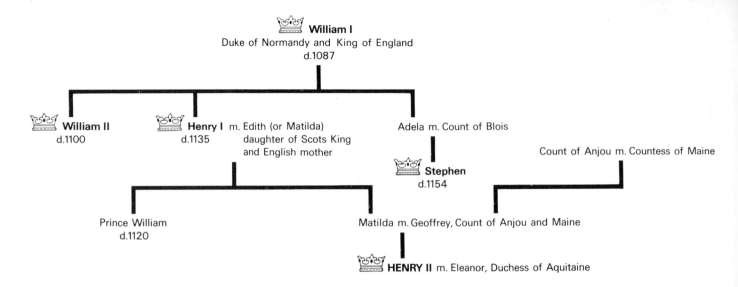

William I
Duke of Normandy and King of England
d.1087

William II
d.1100

Henry I m. Edith (or Matilda)
d.1135   daughter of Scots King
    and English mother

Adela m. Count of Blois

Stephen
d.1154

Count of Anjou m. Countess of Maine

Prince William
d.1120

Matilda m. Geoffrey, Count of Anjou and Maine

HENRY II m. Eleanor, Duchess of Aquitaine

you could easily go a whole day's journey and never find anyone living in a village, nor the land being tilled. Then corn was dear, and meat and butter and cheese, because there was none in the country. Wretched people died of starvation; some lived by begging for alms who had once been rich men; some fled the country.

The trouble, as the chronicler noted, lay partly in Stephen's character. He lacked the ruthlessness that the first three Norman kings had all shown. It was also partly the result of his weak claim to the throne, which brought about civil war. As you can see from the family tree, Stephen was a nephew of the successful and respected King Henry I, who for thirty-five years gave England good, firm government. Henry's only son had been drowned; the *White Ship*, bringing him over from Normandy, had sunk with almost everyone on board when a drunken sailor had steered it on to a rock. But Henry left a daughter, Matilda, and she claimed her father's throne for herself or for her young son, Henry. With civil war raging between those great barons who backed Matilda and those who favoured Stephen, every man of property had to fend for himself. Anyone who could built himself a castle, a motte-and-bailey with stockade and wooden tower set upon a mound. Secure in a base like this he could behave as he liked and obey such laws as he chose.

above: *Alan Sorrell's drawing of a motte-and-bailey castle.*

right: *Berkhamsted Castle, Hertfordshire; a motte-and-bailey with the remains of a shell keep on the motte.*

left: *Part of a page from a thirteenth-century history showing the four Norman kings: William I and William II above, Henry I and Stephen below.*

A thirteenth-century manuscript shows royal justice.

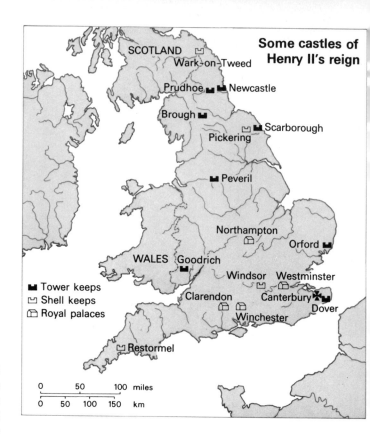

Some castles of Henry II's reign

SCOTLAND
Wark-on-Tweed
Prudhoe · Newcastle
Brough
Pickering · Scarborough
Peveril
Northampton
Orford
WALES · Goodrich
Windsor · Westminster
Clarendon · Canterbury
Winchester · Dover
Restormel

■ Tower keeps
⊔ Shell keeps
⌂ Royal palaces

0   50   100 miles
0   50 100 150   km

Restoring order

Henry was twenty-one, but he already had a reputation as a brave and successful soldier, and most ordinary people were only too happy to see him restoring order. Powerful barons who had used their opportunity to take control of royal castles, or those lesser landowners who had bullied their neighbours, were not so pleased. Henry quickly showed how tough he could be. Troublemakers either mended their ways and behaved peaceably or they were seized by the king's sheriffs and justices and hanged. Those who had built castles without permission had to demolish their walls. Royal castles Henry demanded back at once from those who had occupied them. William le Gros, the powerful Earl of Yorkshire, of whom they said in the north that he was more truly a king than the king himself, was ordered to give up his stronghold on the rocky peninsula of Scarborough, overlooking the North Sea. Only a narrow neck of land flanked by steep cliffs linked it to level ground, and this William had cut with a ditch and guarded with a stone wall so that no one could attack him. William was slow to obey the new king's order. Henry wasted no time. Within days he had gathered an army and was marching north, and when he reached the city of York the earl decided it was wisest to submit without further delay. Scar-

borough was taken over, but though Henry demolished some of the walls that Earl William had set up he decided the site made too good a stronghold to be left unoccupied. Over the next few years the massive stone keep was built that you can see opposite, now much damaged.

Most of the other great nobles quickly followed Earl William's example. Often the king returned their castles to them once they had surrendered, but they were no longer centres of rebellion and disorder. Instead massive royal castles were built across the length and breadth of the country, at Newcastle, Orford and Dover for example. These mighty towers were much more formidable than anything that the greatest noble could afford to build, even if he had been allowed to; and where the king could not set up a stone tower he sometimes strengthened a motte castle by building a stone shell-keep on the mound.

26

Three of Henry's keeps:

right: *Scarborough*

below: *Dover*

below right: *Orford*

Money matters

All this castle-building, and the pay for the castle soldiers as well as for his other soldiers, meant that Henry was soon short of money. The work at Scarborough, for example, cost about £700, and the keep and wall of Newcastle cost £1,144 over ten years. These were enormous sums for the twelfth century, perhaps four or five times the taxes paid by an entire county. In those times the highest paid man in the kingdom, the king's chancellor, earned five shillings a day, and a skilled man might get three pennies for a day's labour.

Henry began by collecting a special *danegeld*, a tax that went back to the days when kings had been forced to buy off Viking raiders. But mostly he relied on the feudal dues from the great landowners, collected by the royal sheriffs. Sometimes the sheriff kept back for his own use rather more of these moneys then he should, so Henry introduced a very strict accounting system. Each sheriff was summoned in turn to Westminster, where the king's treasurer and those barons who worked with him questioned him closely about the money collected from his shire. It was a system that had been started in the days of Henry's grandfather, and the new king made sure that it worked efficiently and smoothly.

One difficulty in the way of keeping proper accounts and checking on the sheriffs' honesty was the system of numbers that the royal clerks had to use. Although some scholars knew about the numbers that Arab mathematicians used, which worked in tens and had a sign for zero (these are the numbers we use today), the treasurer's clerks had only Roman numerals. If you try to add together, say, XLIV shillings, CVI shillings, and XIX shillings, you will find it impossible unless you turn them into modern numbers (44, 106, and 19) or you use a lot of counters. King Henry's ministers had to use counters.

What they did was this. In their room of the royal palace at Westminster they set up a rectangular table covered with a black and white cloth marked with checked squares like a chess board; the table and the clerks who used it came to be known as the *board of the exchequer*. On this counters were placed to represent all the different sums of money the sheriff was due to pay, adding as they went along. Different columns represented different amounts, and the lack of a nought did not matter; there would simply be no counter in that column. Then they could take off counters to represent any payments that the sheriff had made on the king's behalf and at his orders. The final results would be recorded by a clerk on parchment (a prepared sheepskin), and the parchments for the whole year were stitched together and rolled up, so that they resembled a pipe. This was the *Pipe Roll*, and it listed the king's whole income and expenditure. There was little

Tallies, now in the Public Record Office.
Most tallies are between 25 cm and 35 cm long.

Stephen

attempt to sort out the different ways in which money was collected or spent. Money coming from fines and rents and taxes was mixed with money used for castles, soldiers, royal clothes, gifts, and even the king's occasional hot baths.

The sheriff, having handed over the money, needed a receipt. This was given in the form of a tally, a stick of hazel notched to show the amount of payment and then split so that the Exchequer kept one half and the sheriff the other.

Apart from collecting his share of the money in the kingdom, Henry found he needed to do something about the actual coins used throughout his realm. In Stephen's reign it had not been easy to find coins you could trust. No one could be sure that a silver penny would really buy a penny's worth of goods and services, or that there was the right amount of silver in it. Pennies were made not only by the king's own money-makers but also by several of the most powerful barons, and even the royal pennies were produced at many different mints throughout the kingdom. The first two coins above, for example, were made at York. One was made for Stephen and shows him with his queen holding a sceptre between them; the other was made for Eustace fitzJohn and shows him in armour with his sword. Neither of them is very well made. The different money-makers, when they were not firmly under the king's control, might well use poor quality silver for their coins or cut down the weight. So merchants were unwilling to accept coins in exchange for their goods, or would ask more money in order to be safe. Prices rose, much as they have in our own day, and this brought hardship and discontent.

When Henry became king he gathered in most of these poor coins of doubtful quality. Then he issued his own new pennies, just as ugly as the old ones but of a good regular weight and standard pattern that was matched by the mints all over the country. The king made sure that all money-makers pro-

duced good coins or none at all, so once again men trusted the coins, trade improved, and the merchants prospered. Henry, carrying the royal sceptre, appeared on every coin, though it was not a very flattering portrait.

Justice

Too many sheriffs, it seemed to King Henry, were not governing their shires fairly and efficiently. Once again he took up some of the ideas of his grandfather, Henry I, and used them to impose just rule over the whole country. Later in his reign he had no hesitation in removing officials who seemed to have failed at their jobs; but at first he had to rely on many of Stephen's sheriffs, so he did his best to keep a check on their activities.

He used local people. Twelve reliable, law-abiding men were summoned from each division (called a *hundred*) of the shire to report to the king's justices or to the sheriff anyone whom they suspected of robbery or murder, or of helping criminals. The twelve swore that they would tell the truth, and from the Latin word for 'swear' they came to be called a *jury*. Later, similar juries were appointed to settle disputes between landowners.

He also used *justices*, royal servants sent out from his court to administer the king's law throughout the land. The justices would not only examine and sentence criminals presented to them by the juries or the sheriffs, but inquire into local problems, the behaviour of sheriffs, the activities of the great nobles, and the payment of taxes. They reported back to the king, who thus knew what went on throughout his kingdom. At the same time other royal justices remained throughout the year at Westminster to deal with criminals and disputes; they came to be known as justices of the *King's Bench*.

All over the country local knights, landowners and citizens

30

Eustace fitzJohn

These silver pennies are shown at nearly twice their actual size; each is about as big as a new penny.

Henry II

met the king's justices every year when the juries made their reports. It helped to bind together the king and his people, and it began the building of our modern system of local government, by which the people of the countryside share in managing their own affairs.

The Angevin Empire

Henry II ruled not only England but many other territories. His mother was an Anglo-Norman princess, daughter of the Norman Henry I and his English wife. His father, Matilda's husband, had been count of the rich French territory of Anjou. The Count of Anjou's badge was a sprig of yellow broom, which the French called *plante genêt*, and his descendants were known either as Angevins (men of Anjou) or Plantagenets.

North of Anjou was Maine. Its countess had married Henry's Angevin grandfather, so it became joined with Anjou. North again was the Duchy of Normandy, linked to England ever since 1066. Even the civil wars had not broken the link for long, because many a great baron held land in both England and Normandy. Henry was lord of all this, and he also claimed to be overlord of the Kings of Scotland, the Princes of Wales, the Dukes of Brittany and the Counts of Toulouse. Shortly before he became King of England he had added to these lands in a spectacular way by marrying Eleanor, Duchess of Aquitaine, the most celebrated lady of the day, whose lands covered much of southern France. For her territories and many of his own Henry accepted King Louis of France as his overlord; but his lands were far richer and more widespread than those the French king held himself.

It was an enormous 'empire', and it faced Henry with many problems. He was kept forever on the move, fighting the king of France over a border dispute or punishing an unruly baron or besieging a troublesome castle. Henry had, throughout his

reign, to keep order among the lords of Aquitaine at the same time as he was dealing with the troubles of England. He had been born in France and brought up there, he spoke French and wrote Latin but knew no English, and he spent little more than two out of the first eight years of his reign in the English kingdom.

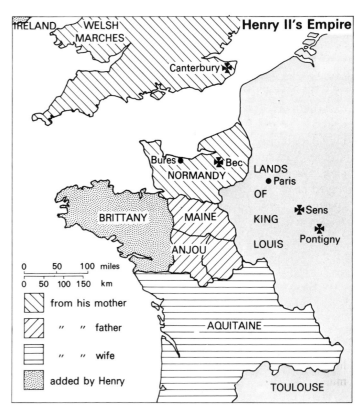

Henry II's Empire

0   50   100 miles
0 50 100 150 km

⊘ from his mother
⧄ " " father
▤ " " wife
░ added by Henry

31

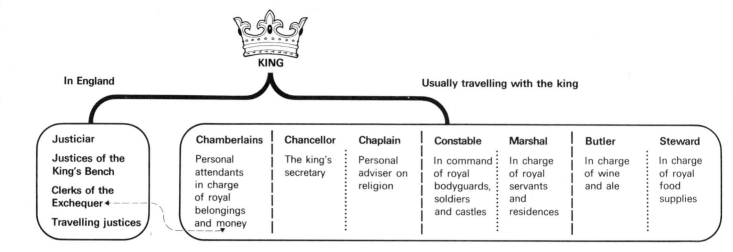

KING

In England | Usually travelling with the king

Justiciar	Chamberlains	Chancellor	Chaplain	Constable	Marshal	Butler	Steward
Justices of the King's Bench Clerks of the Exchequer Travelling justices	Personal attendants in charge of royal belongings and money	The king's secretary	Personal adviser on religion	In command of royal bodyguards, soldiers and castles	In charge of royal servants and residences	In charge of wine and ale	In charge of royal food supplies

Henry's ministers

But if Henry was often away from England, he kept close control over what happened there. Two powerful and trustworthy barons shared the post of *justiciar*, the king's representative in England. Messengers constantly hurried across the Channel between them and the king. A host of other ministers and servants of the king helped in governing the country. Sometimes they were great noblemen, sometimes knights, and sometimes learned clerks who had made their way up from humble beginnings as sons of farmers or tradesmen. Some, like the barons and clerks of the Exchequer, stayed at the king's English palaces of Westminster or Winchester. Others moved with the king about his lands and were always at his elbow.

The king's servants were also his ministers; the same man might attend to his personal wants and to the business of government. There were four main groups of servants.

First, there were the steward and the butler, with their staff. They were mainly concerned with the living and eating arrangements for the king and his court.

Second, the marshal and the constables supervised the king's castles and his soldiers, and arranged the transport of his court from place to place on a herd of pack-horses and mules.

Third, there were the officials of the royal chamber. Because English kings in the past had kept their money close to them, in the royal bedchamber itself, some of the chamber officials became in time lords and clerks of the Exchequer.

Finally, there were the officials of the royal chapel. These included the chaplain, the king's personal adviser in matters of religion. At one time the chaplain had written all the king's letters for him, but since Henry I's day that task had been passed on to a separate official. While the king held his court amid the hurly-burly of his great hall, this official sat with his clerks behind a screen to set down in writing whatever was needed, and from his screen (in Latin, a *cancella*) he took his title, *Chancellor*.

The chancellor had charge of the royal seal. He or the clerk who served him would write out on parchment the king's order (it was called a *writ*) or grant (called a *charter*). Parchment was costly, so the writing would be cramped and there were many abbreviations, as you can see on the opposite page; but a skilful clerk could make the king's wishes perfectly clear in a very brief space. Then one of the clerks would melt a large blob of beeswax, and place it round a cord or a strip of parchment attached to the document. The blob of beeswax would be pressed between two moulds of lead or silver so that the king's great seal, showing Henry as monarch on one side and as warrior knight on the other, proclaimed that the command came with the king's approval and authority. To disobey that command was high treason.

Henry's court on the move

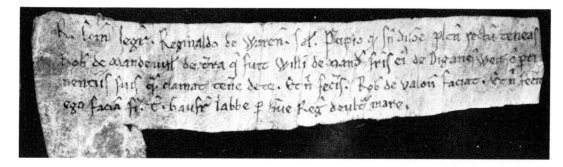

A writ. It is on parchment, about 6 in. (15 cm) wide. This writ was issued by the justiciar in the king's name while Henry was in France. It is in Latin, with many abbreviations. It reads:

Robertus Comes Legrecestrie Reginaldo de Warenna salutem. Precipio quod sine dilatione plenum rectum teneas

Roberto de Mandeuilla de terra que fuit Willelmi de Mandeuilla fratris eius de Diganeswella cum perti-

nenciis suis quam clamat tenere de te. Et nisi feceris, Robertus de Valoniis faciat. Et nisi fecerit,

ego faciam fieri. Teste Gaufrido labbe per breue Regis de ultra mare.

Robert earl of Leicester to Reginald de Warenne greeting. I command that without delay you hold full right to Robert de Mandeville concerning the land which belonged to William de Mandeville his brother of Diganeswell with its appurtenances which he claims to hold of you. And unless you do this, Robert de Valognes is to do it. And unless he does it, I shall cause it to be done. Witness Geoffrey 'l'abbé'. By the king's writ from overseas.

Henry's seal.

The chancellor was the man closest to the king, his secretary, and responsible for seeing all the royal wishes turned into writing. Naturally a good chancellor could save his master much trouble by thinking in advance of what needed to be done. He would have to be someone the king could trust completely, because he would have immense power; and he could get most business done without bothering the king at all.

When Henry arrived from France to take over his new kingdom in December 1154 he found that Archbishop Theobald had been looking after affairs of government since Stephen's death six weeks before. He asked Theobald to find him a good chancellor. Theobald recommended that very efficient archdeacon, Thomas of London.

The king and the chancellor

As chancellor, Thomas was often at his young master's side giving advice, often on important missions, always busy. He, the two justiciars and the old archbishop were the most important men in the kingdom under the king himself. Of the four only Thomas came from amongst the ordinary people, and he was the one most constantly at the king's side as he hurried from place to place to deal with one difficulty after another. At one moment they would be arranging a border dispute with the king of France or planning a marriage between Henry's son and Louis' daughter; at another they would be settling arguments between barons over their rights,

or inquiring into the misdeeds of certain sheriffs. When Henry made war, Thomas collected and paid a force of nearly 2,000 knights and 4,000 footsoldiers and led them to fight for the king. And in time of peace there were always the king's writs to be prepared by the clerks, sealed and despatched.

Henry and Thomas were very different but they worked well together, and they became close friends. Henry was a restless man of action, bothering little about the details of business and ceremony. Thomas, proud of his new importance, loved pomp and display but was also good at office work. He was a merchant's son, and he enjoyed showing his power and wealth to the great nobles whom he invited to dine with him on the finest wine and food from gold and silver dishes. Mere knights often failed to find room on his benches, but he thoughtfully had the floor strewn with fresh straw or rushes every day so that their fine clothes might not be spoiled by sitting on it. But for all his magnificence and the grand clothes he wore, Thomas never forgot that he was a man of the church. He tried to live a good life, and he ate and drank little. Henry, meanwhile, found time to enjoy himself with his usual vigour.

In 1158 Henry sent his chancellor on a special mission to the king of France. Thomas travelled in great style to impress the natives. As William fitzStephen tells us:

He had about two hundred of his household mounted on horseback, including knights, clerks, stewards, serjeants, and sons of nobles, and all in fit array, splendid in new clothes, each according to his rank. He himself had twenty-four changes of clothes, many garments of silk and every kind of fur. He had with him hounds and birds of every kind such as kings and rich men keep.

He had eight waggons, each drawn by five horses, in size and strength like chargers. Each horse had its own groom, young and strong, clad in a new tunic and walking beside the waggon, and each waggon had its driver and guard. Two waggons bore nothing but beer carried in iron-hooped barrels, to be given to the French who admire liquor of this sort, the colour of wine and of better flavour. One waggon was used for the furniture of the chancellor's chapel, one for his private chamber, one for his treasury and another for his kitchen. Twelve packhorses and eight chests carried the chancellor's gold and silver plate, his cups, platters, goblets, pitchers, basins, salt-cellars, salvers and dishes. Each waggon had a dog chained to it, large, fierce and terrible; and on the back of each horse was a long-tailed monkey.

At his entry into the French villages men rushed out of their houses when they heard the din, asking who it was. They were told it was the chancellor of the English king going on embassy to the king of France. Then said the French, 'What a marvellous man the king of England must be if his chancellor travels in such great state.'

Yet when Henry himself visited Paris soon after he travelled hurriedly, with a few companions only.

4 The great quarrel

The enthroning (above left) and the quarrel. These paintings are from Queen Mary's Psalter, made about 1320.

Thomas the archbishop

In 1161 old Archbishop Theobald died. There had been disagreements but on the whole he had worked smoothly with King Henry and his chancellor. Henry wanted someone to replace him who would be equally helpful in the important position of head of the Church. Perhaps he wanted someone who would help to make his control over the Church as complete as his control over the barons and sheriffs and ordinary folk. He turned to the faithful companion who had served him so well over the past seven years. Thomas had been trained in the old archbishop's household. He was a churchman. Though he had never become a priest, he was sincerely religious even if it was not always obvious to outsiders. He could continue to serve Henry loyally in his new post.

Thomas was reluctant to become archbishop. 'I intend to make you Archbishop of Canterbury' said the king, sending him off to England from the castle in Normandy where they had been staying. Thomas smiled, and pointed at the gay and splendid clothes he was wearing. 'How religious, how saintly is the man you want to appoint to that holy task', he replied. And he had a more serious objection. He knew that, as he warned the king, he could serve the Church or the king, but not both. Whoever was made archbishop must soon, it seemed, offend either God or the king.

Henry insisted, and the monks of Canterbury dutifully accepted their new archbishop in June 1162. Thomas was enthroned and consecrated, as shown in the drawing from a richly illustrated book made about 150 years later.

Thomas was right in his fears. To Henry, and to most other people, he seemed to become a changed man. He dedicated his whole life to the service of God and the Church. He wore beneath his robes as archbishop (which are still kept as Sens Cathedral in France) the plain habit of a monk; and beneath that, unknown to anyone until his death, a coarse, uncom

Thomas's chasuble and mitre. They were long kept at Sens Cathedral, but the mitre is now in the Victoria and Albert Museum, London.

fortable horse-hair shirt that kept his body in continual discomfort. He lived the hard life of a monk, filling his days with prayer, and fasting frequently when he was not busy with matters of state. Once he had always been ready to help King Henry. Now, whenever he thought the king was acting wrongly, Thomas was only too ready to speak out against him. In little more than a year he was quarrelling violently with his former master and friend.

The coronations of Edward the Confessor (as painted in the thirteenth century) and (right) of Elizabeth II.

The rights of the Church

Why did the new archbishop quarrel with the king?

Partly it was a personal matter. Henry found that he had made a mistake. He felt bitterly that the man he had honoured with his friendship and a high position had betrayed him, turned against him, ruined his plans. He came to hate Thomas as a traitor. Thomas, for his part, was anxious to prove to all the world, and particularly to the churchmen he now led, and perhaps also to himself, that he was no longer a mere puppet doing the king's bidding.

But the quarrel was also about something much bigger than pride and annoyance. Henry was trying to create a new kind of country. It was to be run firmly and fairly by one man and his servants. Every Englishman owed loyalty to his king and must obey the king's law.

The Church that Thomas now spoke for was also trying to create something new, a new kind of Christian faith that embraced everyone. Every Christian owed loyalty to God and must obey the law of his Church.

So the king and the Church were, sooner or later, bound to clash. But there was nothing new about such a clash. It had happened from time to time throughout the history of Christianity. Perhaps the difficulty began 800 years before Thomas and Henry, when a Roman emperor, Constantine the Great, decided to stop treating Christians as a dangerous nuisance (as earlier emperors had) and got them on to his own side. From then on Christians had become loyal supporters of the Roman Empire, and Christian bishops helped Roman governors. In return the emperor favoured Christianity above all the other religions of Rome, and made it the official religion. Many other rulers later adopted the same idea. Kings would promise their help to the Church, and make sure their subjects were good Christians. In return, they expected the Church to show all their Christian people that it approved of the king; so an archbishop would take part in the coronation, anointing the new ruler with holy oil and perhaps even placing the crown on his head. This has been done by the Archbishop of Canterbury for English kings since Anglo-Saxon times, and it is done still.

This was a good arrangement, king and archbishop working together, just as they did in the days of William I and Lanfranc. But Lanfranc's actions had begun the changes in the English Church that made people, and priests in particular, think much more about religion. There were fine new churches now throughout England. There were keen parish priests filled with new ideas. There were scholars eagerly debating the importance of the Church. There were a host of new monasteries, great strongholds of religion like Fountains and Rievaulx; about 5,000 monks lived in England by Thomas's day, in 300 monasteries; a hundred years before there had been only 850 monks in 35 monasteries. Everywhere, in the middle of the twelfth century, Christianity seemed alive and important.

The same thing was happening in many Christian lands; all over Europe bishops quarrelled with lords, archbishops with kings, and popes with emperors. Full of zeal for their faith churchmen questioned the rights of a ruler who knew nothing of the new religious learning to interfere.

Henry wanted to be sure that the right people were running the English Church. He had made the great barons obey him. He could not see why the Church, too, should not obey him as it had obeyed his great-grandfather. Archbishop Thomas soon showed that he was not going to obey, that indeed he was only too ready to annoy the king.

Soon after his enthronement Thomas found that certain castles once belonging to Canterbury had fallen into the hands of powerful nobles, and he speedily demanded his rights. An important lord named William, a tenant of the king, had named a new vicar for his village of Eynsford. Thomas held that he was wrong to do so; he, as archbishop, should have appointed the vicar. It was a small matter, but when William argued Thomas punished him in the most terrible way he could; he *excommunicated* him, drove him out of the Christian Church, which meant that he could never hope for salvation in the after-life. Henry was annoyed, because William naturally appealed to his overlord for help, and the king had to ask Thomas to lift the sentence. Then there was a council where the archbishop picked a quarrel with the king over money matters that were really, Henry felt, none of his business.

But the worst disagreement was over *criminous clerks*.

Any clerk, that is almost anyone who had a smattering of education, could claim to be a member of the Church. As a member of the Church, he could be tried for a criminal offence only by a Church court, presided over by a bishop, and not by the king's court, presided over by a sheriff or justice. The king's courts might sentence an offender to death or mutilation. The Church courts would sentence him only to show his repentance by doing *penance*, by fasting, perhaps, or going on pilgrimage.

In 1163 a priest named Philip de Brois was accused of the murder of a knight but acquitted by the Bishop of Lincoln's court. The Sheriff of Bedfordshire summoned him to stand trial again; Philip not only refused to appear but insulted the sheriff into the bargain. The sheriff reported to the king, who ordered that Philip should be tried again. Thomas, however, had Philip tried in his own court, and again acquitted him, though in an effort to please the king he handed the priest over for a flogging because he had insulted the king's sheriff. But he insisted that no clerk be tried by the king's justices.

Henry was furious. Making enquiries, he found that more than a hundred clerks were said to have committed murder since the beginning of his reign, and he did not think they should get away with it.

Then Henry made an unfortunate mistake, perhaps because he had no shrewd chancellor at his side to advise him. He had his clerks set down in writing just what he considered his powers as king were, and he ordered the bishops to agree.

The site of Clarendon.

The Constitutions of Clarendon

The king had a palace, a stone and timber hall, on the edge of his New Forest hunting ground at Clarendon. Nothing of it stands now, though its foundations can be seen from the air. Here he summoned all the bishops in the middle of January 1164, demanding that they should accept what were called the Constitutions of Clarendon:

Henry said:

1 *Bishops can only be elected if the king approves, and they should swear loyalty to the king.*

2 *Too many criminals are claiming to be churchmen and wanting to be tried by Church courts, which let them off lightly. They must be handed over to the king's courts for proper punishment. Moreover, any dispute over property between a layman and a churchman should be settled by the king's courts.*

3 *Too many churchmen, dissatisfied with the justice they get here, are going off to Rome to appeal to the pope. They must not leave the country or appeal to the pope without the king's consent.*

4 *The bishops are too ready to use the fearsome weapon of excommunication, driving men who upset them out of the Church altogether so that they are cut off from God and face eternal damnation. There must be no excommunication of great lords or of the king's ministers without the king's consent.*

The bishops answered:

We accept. This is the way things are done in England, because the bishops are great lords as well as churchmen.

But only Church courts can judge churchmen fairly, and no man should be punished twice for one offence, by both Church court and royal court.

But the pope is head of the whole Christian Church, and churchmen must always be free to seek his advice and help. In these matters the judgement of the head of the Church is sounder than that of the head of the country.

But only the Church can decide who has sinned so gravely that they must be driven from it. The Church must protect itself from its enemies.

So the bishops, led by Thomas, agreed to some of the king's demands but were united against most of them. Henry was determined, and he brought a lot of pressure to bear on Thomas. Even the pope, who wanted to keep on friendly terms with Henry, advised the archbishop to accept the king's demands; but that was before the pope heard the full details of what Henry wanted.

Under pressure, Thomas also made a mistake. He accepted the Constitutions of Clarendon, and all the other bishops followed him. Almost at once he changed his mind; but it was too late now for the others to follow him and act together. United, they might have forced the king to change some of his demands; but most of the bishops now decided it was better to co-operate with the king. They accepted the lead of Thomas's enemies, the Archbishop of York and the Bishop of London.

Thomas was annoyed with himself and sought the advice of the pope. The king was furious, for this seemed a deliberate breach of the Constitutions. He summoned Thomas to appear before him at Northampton to explain his behaviour. When he arrived the archbishop found himself faced with charges that he had not only ignored the king's wishes but also that in his days as chancellor he had kept large sums of money to which he had no right. After days of wrangling, the king ordered the earl of Leicester to pronounce sentence. Thomas refused to listen. He swept out angrily, with the king's barons and servants surging around him shouting 'Traitor'. He knew all too well what Henry's temper was like and he quickly fled in a small boat to France. It was November 1164, and he was to remain in exile for six years.

The exile

Thomas hurried to the pope to tell his story. The pope sympathized, although he was anxious if possible to restore friendly relations between king and archbishop.

Thomas sailing into exile, from Queen Mary's Psalter.

Henry showed his annoyance in a number of ways. When Thomas went to live in a Cistercian monastery at Pontigny, the king threatened to seize the property of all the Cistercian monasteries in England unless he was driven out; so Thomas had to move on to the town of Sens, where a fine new cathedral was just being completed. Henry wrote to King Louis begging him not to harbour a man guilty of infamous crimes and treasons, but Louis was in no hurry to solve his powerful neighbour's problems. Henry was reduced to driving out of the country the archbishop's relations and those of his clerks who supported him, and confiscating all their property. He seized all the lands and possessions of Canterbury itself, handing some to men who had always been enemies of the archbishop.

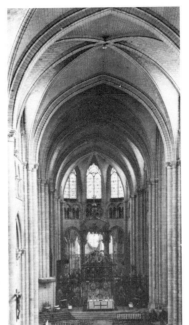

above: *Pontigny Abbey.*

right: *Sens Cathedral, the east end, inside and outside.*

Thomas did nothing to make matters better. He solemnly excommunicated some of the king's supporters and advisers, and all who had taken Canterbury property. He can be seen in this drawing from a French manuscript of the thirteenth century as, before a great crowd, he goes through the dreadful ceremony that will drive his enemies out of God's Church. It ends with Thomas taking up the candles about him, turning them upside down, and dashing them to the ground.

He threatened to go further, to call upon the pope to place all England under an *interdict*, which would close all the churches and leave everyone without the help of a priest.

He wrote to the king, but his words can only have made Henry even more angry with this upstart whom, as he now bitterly regretted, he had raised from the gutter. 'With great

Thomas's return in 1170, from a thirteenth-century French manuscript.

longing', Thomas wrote, 'I have desired to see your face again and speak with you. In that you are my lord I owe and offer you my advice and service; in that you are my king, I am bound to respect and admire you.' All was well so far, but then he went on: 'In that you are my spiritual son, I am bound by my post to chasten and correct you. Since it is certain that kings receive their power from the Church, not the Church from them but from Christ, so you have no power to give rules to bishops, to judge Church matters. Listen to the advice of your subject, to the warnings of your bishop, to the correction of your father. Restore everything that has been forcibly taken from myself or my servants, and allow us a safe and peaceful return. Otherwise you can be sure that you shall feel the full weight of God's severity and punishment.'

The return

King Louis and the pope made several attempts to bring the two men together. Once Thomas even promised to obey the king, but then he spoiled it by adding 'save for the honour of God', meaning that he would do nothing he thought harmful to the Church.

In 1170 the quarrel was at last patched up. King Henry decided that his eldest son, young Henry, was old enough to be crowned right away. There was room for two kings in his vast empire, and having the next king already accepted might lessen the danger of civil war when he died.

Henry got Thomas's old rival the Archbishop of York to perform the crowning ceremony. Yet by long tradition only the Archbishop of Canterbury might crown a king of England. Both Thomas and the pope himself were so annoyed by this step that they threatened to put the country under an interdict. With the danger of every church in the land being closed, Henry agreed to allow the archbishop to return to Canterbury. Early in December Thomas at last came back to his cathedral, welcomed (as this thirteenth-century drawing shows) by many of the common people.

But Thomas was determined to punish those churchmen who, he felt, had deserted him and betrayed their Church. He would not withdraw the excommunication with which he had threatened all those who had taken part in young Henry's coronation, and he warned of more excommunications unless all its properties were returned to Canterbury. The Archbishop of York, with the Bishop of London and another excommunicated churchman, hurried off to Normandy to complain to King Henry that Thomas was still pursuing his trouble-making path.

It was when he heard these tales that King Henry lost his temper once again. This time the result was fatal.

5 Saint Thomas

Some people in his lifetime thought of Archbishop Thomas as the brave defender of all good Christian people against the might of an overbearing king. Others thought him a cantankerous, ungrateful upstart obstructing a hard-working ruler. Some thought the quarrel was about general ideas: ancient rights, the freedom of the Church, royal power, good government. Others regarded it as a personal disagreement. Different people held different views of Thomas's behaviour in his lifetime; and it is still possible to hold these different views today.

But immediately after the archbishop's death almost everyone agreed that he had been brutally murdered by a man who had no respect for God's Church; therefore he was a martyr. Within hours of the murder, as the monks hurriedly buried Thomas in the crypt (as shown in the painting on the right, made twenty or thirty years afterwards), they found what was to them startling evidence of his saintliness: the scratchy, louse-ridden hair-shirt that he had so long worn next to his skin. Clearly the archbishop had never enjoyed the comfortable life that had been apparent to outsiders. He had deliberately made himself suffer.

Then miracles were reported, a sure proof of saintliness. A monk saw Thomas apparently restored to life in a dream. A woman who prayed to the martyr was promptly cured of blindness. Those who had scraped up drops of Thomas's blood told of all kinds of ailments and injuries cured. They believed passionately that the dead archbishop would help them, and their confidence was often rewarded. Then men knew for certain that he was a holy martyr and, as the pope officially announced two years later, a saint.

The pilgrims

From that time on all who sought help from the Church in this world or the next tried to secure the assistance of Saint Thomas of Canterbury. They could best do this by making their way to his tomb on pilgrimage. Fifty years after the murder, Saint Thomas's remains were moved to a new tomb behind the high altar, a splendid tomb fittingly plated with gold, where the prior himself would point out to distinguished visitors the many magnificent jewels adorning it, and explain what king or prince or great lord had given each.

This new tomb had an appropriate setting. Since Thomas's cathedral was soon destroyed by fire, the monks set to work to create a new building worthy to hold the relics of the saint. They called in a French architect named William of Sens, who had worked on the cathedral where Thomas had stayed during his exile; and William began the building in a style completely new to England. His pointed arches replaced the round, heavy Norman style, his columns looked slender and elegant, and his windows tall and narrow. It was the first great English building in what we now call the *Gothic* style.

The tall pointed windows in the chapel at the east end of the cathedral, about Thomas's tomb, were filled with richly coloured glass. The windows told the story of Saint Thomas, and of the many miracles that had occurred since his death. They showed, for example, pilgrims visiting the first tomb, down in the crypt, to touch the saint's remains through the holes in its side.

Opposite, you can see how the steps up to the tomb were worn hollow by the feet of pilgrims over hundreds of years. The Black Prince was buried on one side of Thomas, King Henry IV with his queen on the other. In an age when many folk never travelled far from their homes, the journey to Canterbury was the only one that some people ever made.

far left: *The choir.*
left: *View from the south east. The towers were added later.*
below left: *The pilgrim steps.*
right: *Pilgrims at the tomb in the crypt, from one of the windows.*

A pilgrim's badge, made of pewter in the early fourteenth century.

Three of the pilgrims from Chaucer's Canterbury Tales, as they were drawn for the copy of the poem that was printed by William Caxton.

They would proudly wear the lead or pewter souvenirs of their visit, like that above. For many pilgrims, the trip became a holiday, perhaps the only one in a hard-working life. The pilgrims that Geoffrey Chaucer rode with in 1388, and whose tales he retold in the greatest English poem of the Middle Ages, seemed to be out to enjoy themselves. Their bridles carried jingling 'Canterbury Bells', and the trotting of their horses came to be known as a 'Canterbury Gallop', or canter.

The king's penance

Henry, of course, was deeply distressed over what had happened. It was, he explained, a tragic mistake; but he realised that he must take some of the blame. Perhaps he was rather relieved that the troublesome Thomas was gone, but he had to promise to make amends. He undertook to return all the Canterbury property, to give up the claim to punish criminous clerks, and to go off on crusade to the Holy Land. And he promised that he would himself visit Saint Thomas's tomb to suffer penance, punishment for his share in the crime.

In time, three and a half years after the murder, Henry did go to Canterbury, though he got out of going on crusade. He arrived humble and barefoot, and allowed himself to be whipped by all the monks. He was the more ready to show his regret in this way because ever since the death of Thomas things had

Henry's penance, in a fifteenth-century window from an Oxfordshire church.

gone badly for him; there was rebellion throughout the land, made worse by an invading army from Scotland rampaging through Northumberland. It really seemed as though God was punishing Henry for his crime.

It was probably just a stroke of luck that, as he was going through his painful whipping, some of Henry's soldiers far away in the north came by chance on the King of Scots resting with a few knights of his invading army. There was a short, sharp fight, and the king was a prisoner in English hands; the danger from Scotland was over. This spectacular success made it clear, Henry claimed, that Saint Thomas and God had forgiven him and were once more on his side.

Henry was able to avoid further trouble with the Church. He avoided upsetting churchmen, he was careful not to put too many demands in writing, and he found a reliable and peaceful new archbishop for Canterbury. By moving cautiously he got the co-operation he needed from the Church. His son John was not so careful. He became king in 1199 and was soon faced with an archbishop, Stephen Langton, who deliberately modelled his behaviour on that of Saint Thomas, so that quarrelling started all over again.

The end of the quarrel

The long quarrels of king and Church were finally settled when another Henry came to the throne 300 years later. At the same time pilgrimages to Canterbury and the adoration of the relics of Saint Thomas came to an end. Henry VIII was a much more ruthless king than Henry II, and when he quarrelled with the Church he had no hesitation in shattering its structure, destroying its defenders, and remaking it to suit himself. He could not face the thought that many of his subjects worshipped the memory and relics of a churchman who had defied an earlier Henry, and moreover he was short of money. Thomas was no saint, Henry proclaimed, and his images painted on church walls or set in glass must be destroyed. The magnificent shrine was broken up, the bones scattered, and twenty-six cartloads of treasure were removed from Canterbury for the king.

Thomas's shrine is gone, but the cathedral that was built around it still stands and many who admire Thomas Becket as a good and brave man still go there to honour him. The story of archbishop and king has another interest now, and the conflict of these two men has become a favourite theme for those who write novels and plays. Lord Tennyson, Queen

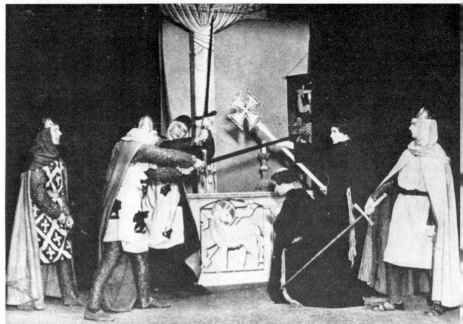

Henry Irving as Becket; right: Murder in the Cathedral *in London, 1936;* below left: *The film of Anouilh's* Becket, *with Richard Burton.*

Victoria's poet laureate, made a rather fanciful play around the story of the proud churchman and his king, and the part of Becket was a favourite with Sir Henry Irving, the greatest actor of his day. In 1935 another poet, T. S. Eliot, wrote *Murder in the Cathedral*, to be produced in the very building where it had happened. It has become accepted as one of the greatest and most moving plays of modern times; not only has it some splendid poetry, but it helps us to understand the kind of thoughts that must have worried Thomas as he waited for a death that he half welcomed, half dreaded. *Murder in the Cathedral* was made into a film, and so was *Becket*, by the French dramatist Jean Anouilh, which returned to the story of two quarrelling personalities and got most of the facts completely wrong.

Whether the story of the archbishop and the king is just about two men and their disagreements, or about conflict between Church and state, freedom and tyranny, old ways and new, it is a story that will be told and retold time and again in many different ways.